On the
Wild Side

Contents

Features

There are many people helping to look after Earth's environment and wildlife. Find out about some of these people in Earth Watch.

How safe are chemicals that people use to kill pests? Read about DDT on page 9 and then decide for yourself.

An animal is extinct when none of its kind can be found anywhere, but what is an endangered or threatened animal? Turn to page 13 to find out.

What kind of vehicle can fly underwater? Discover more in **Flying Beneath the Waves** on page 21.

What is the World Wildlife Fund?

Visit www.rigbyinfoquest.com
for more about ENVIRONMENTAL GROUPS.

On the Wild Side

Since the 1800s, people have made many improvements to their lives. They have invented machines to help them move and work faster. They have learned to harvest Earth's resources. However, some of these changes have caused damage to Earth's oceans, forests, and animals.

Rachel Carson, Eugène Rutagarama, Dr. Sylvia Earle, and Peter Garrett are **environmentalists.** They have each worked hard, in many different ways, to help look after the world's natural environment. Sometimes, they have had to speak up and "walk on the wild side" to have their causes heard!

Key to Environmentalists

Rachel Carson, U.S.A., fought against the use of chemicals in the environment.

Eugène Rutagarama, Rwanda, is helping to save the mountain gorilla population in central Africa.

Dr. Sylvia Earle, U.S.A., studies and explores the world's oceans and ocean life.

Peter Garrett, Australia, is working to protect Australia's rivers, national parks, and oceans.

On the following pages, you will read about the work of environmentalists, such as Sir Peter Blake, from many parts of the world. These people work to help save Earth's environment and wildlife.

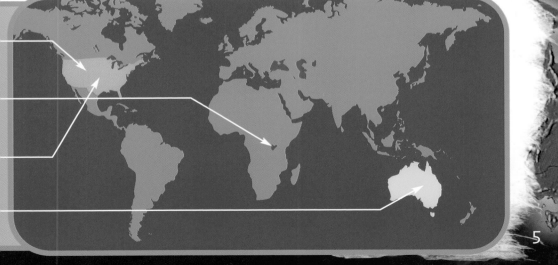

Rachel Carson

Who Was Rachel Carson?

Rachel Carson was born in the United States in 1907. As a young girl, Rachel loved to write stories. As a young woman, Rachel studied at a university and then at a **marine laboratory.** It was at the laboratory that she became interested in the world's oceans and the environment.

Throughout her career, Rachel combined her love of writing with her love of the environment. She wrote three books about her ocean studies. Then, in 1962, she wrote *Silent Spring.* People still talk about this book today.

Rachel Carson's Life

1907—Born in Springdale, Pennsylvania, U.S.A.

1936—Wrote science radio scripts, then became Editor-in-Chief of all publications for the U.S. Fish and Wildlife Service

1941—First book, *Under the Sea-Wind*, published

1945—Became aware of effects of chemicals in the environment

1962—*Silent Spring* published

1963—Called for new government policies to protect human health and the environment. Presented her ideas to Congress (below)

1964—Died in Silver Spring, Maryland, U.S.A.

1999—Named one of *Time* magazine's "Top 20 Most **Influential** Scientists and Thinkers of the Twentieth Century"

What Did Rachel Carson Do?

While studying the oceans, Rachel noticed the effects of **pesticides** on the environment. She questioned some scientists in chemical businesses about the long-term dangers of using pesticides. This was the subject of her book *Silent Spring.*

"There was a strange stillness. The birds, for example, where had they gone? It was a spring without voices. On the mornings that had once throbbed with the dawn chorus of robins, catbirds, doves, jays, wrens, and scores of other voices, there was now no sound; only silence lay over the fields and woods and marsh."

from *Silent Spring,* Rachel Carson, 1962

Many business people were angry about the book before it was published. However, U.S. President John F. Kennedy was very interested in Rachel's writing. He ordered studies on the effects of pesticides. By the end of 1962, **bills** had been introduced in many states to control the use of pesticides.

WHAT'S YOUR OPINION?

A chemical called DDT was made in the 1940s and used in wartime to kill insects that spread disease. By doing this, DDT saved millions of human lives. However, when people started to use it widely, sometimes in their own backyards, birds and fish began to die. Although DDT is now banned in many parts of the world, some countries still use it. What do you think about this? Should there be a worldwide ban on DDT? Why or why not?

Spraying crops with chemicals can get rid of unwanted pests. However, some people believe that pesticides can be harmful to people and animals.

The Environment

SAVING THE AMAZON

The Amazon rain forest is the largest tropical forest in the world. But every day, trees are cut down and land is cleared.

Chico Mendes (1944–1988) was a rubber tapper who worked in the Amazon rain forest. His job of collecting rubber did not destroy any trees. When he saw other people destroying parts of the forest, he decided to do something about it. He traveled the world to talk about the destruction of the rain forest. He helped people learn about problems in the forest.

Today, there are still many people working to help save the Amazon rain forest.

Amazon Basin

WORKING IN THE ARCTIC

Monte Hummel is President of the World Wildlife Fund (WWF) in Canada.

His lifelong interest in the environment began when he returned to his childhood home in Ontario, Canada, to find a poisoned river and the local community in despair.

Today, Monte's special interest is in the Arctic, where WWF has been working for more than 25 years. The Arctic is home to many animals, including polar bears and whales. WWF's main goals in the Arctic are to protect the animals and their homes and to reduce the amount of poisons in the environment.

The Arctic

Eugène Rutagarama

Who Is Eugène Rutagarama?

Eugène Rutagarama was born in Rwanda, Africa, in 1955. He is a **conservationist** with a special interest in saving mountain gorillas. In 1991, he was forced to leave his country because of a war.

AFRICA

Democratic Republic of Congo

Uganda

Rwanda

Eugène's love of animals led him to risk his life and return to Rwanda. He traveled many times to dangerous areas, taking money and supplies to park rangers. In 2001, Eugène was one of six people who won an important environmental award (shown right) for his work.

Mountain gorillas are an endangered species. The word *endangered* is used to describe a kind of animal that is in danger of becoming extinct. The word *threatened* is used to describe animals that are likely to become endangered in the near future, especially if some of the conditions in their environment are not changed.

What Does Eugène Rutagarama Do?

Eugène has spent many years helping protect the world's remaining mountain gorillas. In his job as Program Manager for the International Gorilla Conservation Program (IGCP), Eugène works in the African countries of Rwanda, Uganda, and the Democratic Republic of Congo.

Closely tracking the number of gorillas left in the wild is an important part of protecting these animals. So is making sure that both the local people and the leaders of Rwanda understand the environmental problems affecting the gorillas.

What is the World Wildlife Fund?

Visit www.rigbyinfoquest.com
for more about ENVIRONMENTAL GROUPS.

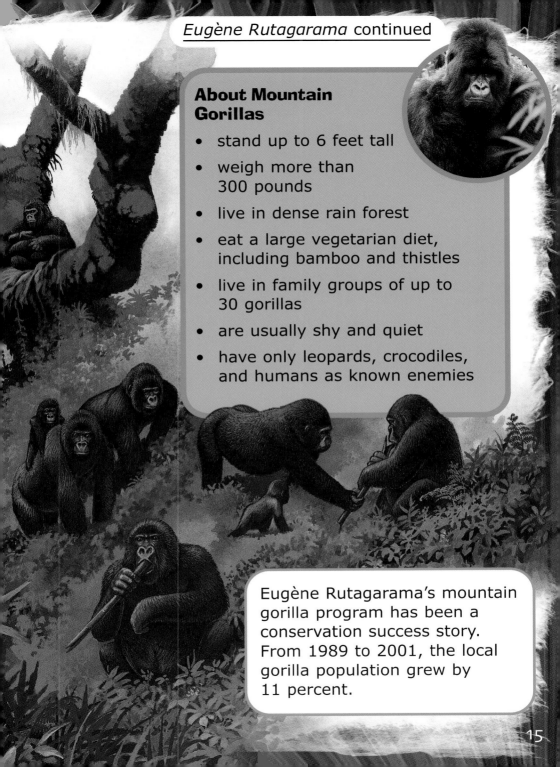

About Mountain Gorillas

- stand up to 6 feet tall
- weigh more than 300 pounds
- live in dense rain forest
- eat a large vegetarian diet, including bamboo and thistles
- live in family groups of up to 30 gorillas
- are usually shy and quiet
- have only leopards, crocodiles, and humans as known enemies

Eugène Rutagarama's mountain gorilla program has been a conservation success story. From 1989 to 2001, the local gorilla population grew by 11 percent.

Wildlife Workers

THE FASTEST ANIMAL ON LAND

Laurie Marker is Director of the Cheetah Conservation Fund (CCF) in Namibia, Africa. Cheetahs are the world's fastest land animals. They are facing extinction in Africa. Before CCF worked in Africa, game wardens and farmers protected their livestock by killing cheetahs found hunting for food inside fenced land. Now, because of CCF's work, cheetahs are captured in traps, cared for by Laurie, and then returned to the wild.

Namibia

NO TIME TO FEED

Dr. Ian Stirling is a scientist and polar bear expert who works for the Canadian Wildlife Service.

His recent studies have shown that there are fewer and fewer polar bears left in the wild. Their icy feeding ground is melting earlier each year because of climate changes caused by **global warming**. The bears are forced from the ice and their feeding time is cut short. Scientists have found that the bears are much lighter and thinner than they should be.

SCALE FOR RATING POLAR BEARS

1	2	3	4	5
skeleton-like, sick or starving	thin, spine visible, little fat	average amount of fat	very fat	obese, body almost round

A rating of 5 is healthy for a polar bear. Today, there are many more bears at the lower end of the scale than in the past.

Dr. Sylvia Earle

Who Is Dr. Sylvia Earle?

Dr. Sylvia Earle was born in the United States in 1935. She is a leading **oceanographer** who was one of the first underwater explorers to use scuba-diving equipment.

Sylvia's first scuba dive was at the age of 17. Since then, she has had many exciting underwater adventures. She was one of the first female oceanographers to live in an underwater chamber. There, she studied habitats in the sea for 14 days. She also helped design the first **submersibles** to go as deep as 3,000 feet.

Sylvia says that every creature she has met in the ocean has a personality all its own.

What Does Dr. Sylvia Earle Do?

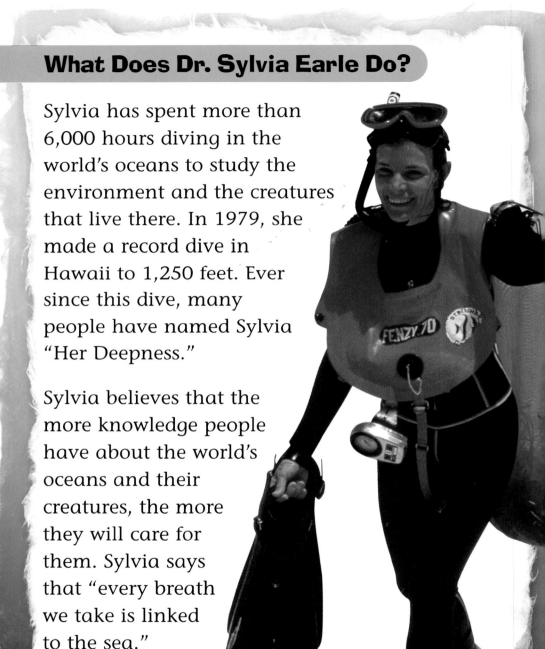

Sylvia has spent more than 6,000 hours diving in the world's oceans to study the environment and the creatures that live there. In 1979, she made a record dive in Hawaii to 1,250 feet. Ever since this dive, many people have named Sylvia "Her Deepness."

Sylvia believes that the more knowledge people have about the world's oceans and their creatures, the more they will care for them. Sylvia says that "every breath we take is linked to the sea."

Believe it or not, this is not an underwater astronaut! It is actually Sylvia inside a special diving suit called a Jim Suit.

TECHTALK

Flying Beneath the Waves

1996
Deep Flight 1, an experimental one-person submersible, was built to prove that underwater flight was possible.

1997
Wet Flight, a one-person submersible, was designed for underwater filming.

In the Future...
A vehicle may be built to go as deep as 36,000 feet—to the bottom of the ocean's deepest trench.

EARTH WATCH

Ocean Explorers

THE UNDERSEA WORLD

Captain Jacques Cousteau (1910–1997) was a French ocean explorer, environmentalist, author, and movie producer. He spent many years exploring the world's oceans and writing and making movies about his discoveries.

On his research ship *Calypso*, he filmed a television series that was popular throughout the world. It helped to educate people about the fascinating world beneath the sea and the need to conserve ocean life.

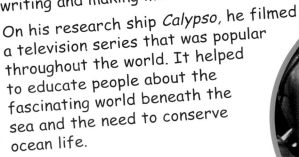

SAILING THE SEAS

Sir Peter Blake (1948–2001) was a New Zealand sailor who won many major world yachting races.

In 2000, he formed an environmental organization called *blakexpeditions*. The goal was to teach people about protecting life in, on, and around the oceans of the world. A Web site was set up so people all over the world could follow the voyages of the exploration boat *Seamaster*. Sadly, Sir Peter Blake was killed in the Amazon Basin in 2001, but his work is being carried on today.

Peter Garrett

Who Is Peter Garrett?

Peter Garrett grew up in Sydney, Australia, in the 1950s and 1960s. His interest in the environment began when he discovered that the forest he had explored as a child was disappearing and the ocean he loved to surf was becoming polluted.

Peter Garrett is now the lead singer of an Australian band called Midnight Oil. The band is as well known for its support of the environment as it is for its music. Peter joined the band in 1977 after finishing a law degree. Many of Midnight Oil's lyrics are about the environment.

Cool wind, clear my head.
Bright sun, grow my food.
Strong rain, clear my heart.
Fill my land. It's a new day.

"Bushfire," written by Peter Garrett, performed by Midnight Oil. From the album *Earth and Sun and Moon.*

What Does Peter Garrett Do?

Peter Garrett was President of the Australian Conservation Foundation (ACF) from 1989 to 1993. He left ACF to work for Greenpeace, another conservation group. After five years, Peter left Greenpeace to become President of the Australian Conservation Foundation once more.

One of the ACF's most important goals is to protect Australia's coasts and marine areas. Other goals include saving Australia's national parks and bringing life back to the once mighty Murray, Darling, and Snowy Rivers.

Save the Snowy

When a dam was built on the Snowy River in 1967, it almost completely stopped the flow of water. The fast-flowing, wild river became choked with weeds and sand.

Finally in February 2001, local governments agreed to add water to the river to increase and restore the flow. A program such as this happens in stages over about ten years.

AUSTRALIA

Snowy River

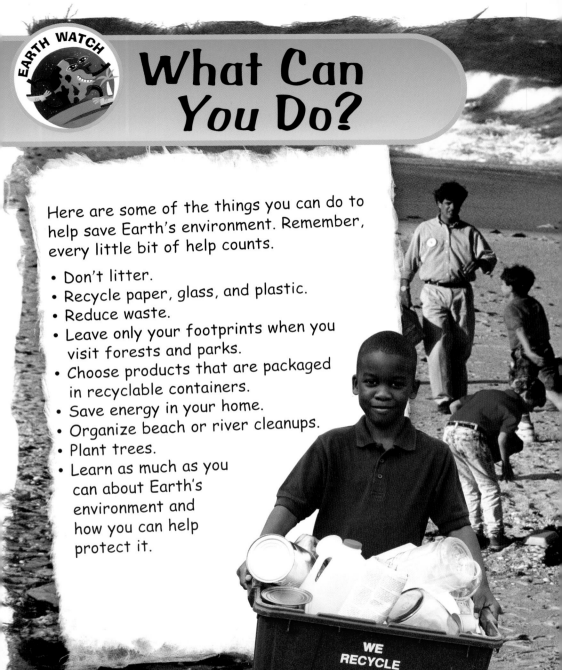

What Can You Do?

Here are some of the things you can do to help save Earth's environment. Remember, every little bit of help counts.

- Don't litter.
- Recycle paper, glass, and plastic.
- Reduce waste.
- Leave only your footprints when you visit forests and parks.
- Choose products that are packaged in recyclable containers.
- Save energy in your home.
- Organize beach or river cleanups.
- Plant trees.
- Learn as much as you can about Earth's environment and how you can help protect it.

WE RECYCLE

Many countries celebrate Earth Day and Arbor Day each year. On Earth Day, communities and groups around the world organize activities that help people learn about caring for the environment. Arbor Day is a day especially set aside for planting trees.

You and your friends or classmates can organize beach or river cleanups.

Glossary

bill – a written plan for a new law that is presented to Congress. A bill needs to be discussed and agreed on before it can be passed as law.

conservationist – a person who is concerned about caring for and protecting wildlife, forests, water, and other natural resources

environmentalist – a person who is concerned about protecting the world's natural environment

global warming – climate changes caused when the gases of burning coal and oil are trapped in Earth's atmosphere, making Earth warmer

influential – having power and knowledge that can change the way other people think or act

marine laboratory – a place that is specially set up for scientists to study oceans and ocean life

oceanographer – a scientist whose work involves the world's oceans and the plants and animals that live there. There are many different parts of the oceans to study, from the surfaces to the ocean floors.

pesticide – a chemical that is used to kill pests in the environment. Pesticides are often used to kill insects that eat crops.

submersible – a small submarine that can go as deep as seven miles beneath an ocean's surface

Index

Bibliography

Carson, Rachel. *The Sea.* MacGibbon & Kee Ltd., 1964.

Carson, Rachel. *Silent Spring.* Hamish Hamilton Ltd., 1962.

Earle, Sylvia A. *Sea Change.* G. P. Putnam's Sons, 1995.

Goodall, Jane. *Beyond Innocence.* Houghton Mifflin Company, 2001.

Montgomery, Sy. *Walking with the Great Apes.* Houghton Mifflin Company, 1991.

Stirling, Ian. *Polar Bears.* The University of Michigan Press, 1988.

Discussion Starters

1 Does your country have a list of animals that are threatened or endangered? Find out as much as you can about your country's native animals. If there is a kind of animal that is at risk, can you think of anything you can do to help its survival?

2 If you could choose to work with one of the people talked about in this book, who would it be? Why?

3 Do you know of any environmentalists who are working in your community? What do they do? How could you help? See if you can find out about other local environmentalists.